SEA LIFE

JELLYFISH

by **Mari Schuh**

raintree

a Capstone company — publishers for children

Raintree is an imprint of Capstone Global Library Limited, a company incorporated in England and Wales having its registered office at 7 Pilgrim Street, London, EC4V 6LB – Registered company number: 6695582

www.raintree.co.uk
myorders@raintree.co.uk

Editorial Credits
Elizabeth R. Johnson, editor; Aruna Rangarajan, designer;
Kelly Garvin, media researcher; Tori Abraham, production specialist

ISBN 978 1 4747 0479 3
19 18 17 16 15
10 9 8 7 6 5 4 3 2 1

British Library Cataloguing in Publication Data
A full catalogue record for this book is available from the British Library.

Photo Credits
Corbis/Ingo Arndt, 19; iStockphoto/mauinov_____, 11; Shutterstock: dibrova, 13, Ethan Daniels, 5, Godruma, cove_____ Rattanko, 7, Richard A. McMIllin, 15, Vlad61, 17

Design Elements: Shutterstock: Jiri Vaclavek, _____

Every effort has been made to contact copyrig_____ missions will be rectified in subsequent printings if notice is given to th_____

All the Internet addresses (URLs) given in thi_____ er, due to the dynamic nature of the Internet, some addresses may ha_____ xist since publication. While the author and publisher regret any inc_____ or any such changes can be accepted by either the author or the publisher.

Printed in China

Contents

Life in the sea 4

Up close 8

Finding food 14

Life cycle 18

Glossary 22

Read more 23

Websites 23

Index 24

Life in the sea

Jellyfish are not what they seem.
Do not let their name fool you.
Jellyfish are not fish at all!

Jellyfish are sea animals.
They float in seas and
oceans around the world.

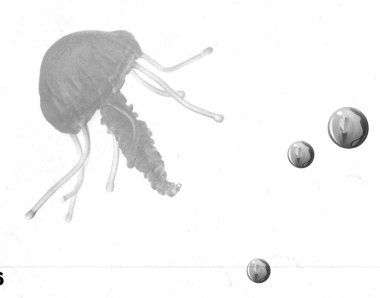

Up close

Jellyfish are many sizes.

Some are as small as a pea.

Others are bigger than a human.

They can be 2 metres wide.

Bright colours cover some jellyfish.
Other jellyfish are clear.
Some jellyfish even glow!

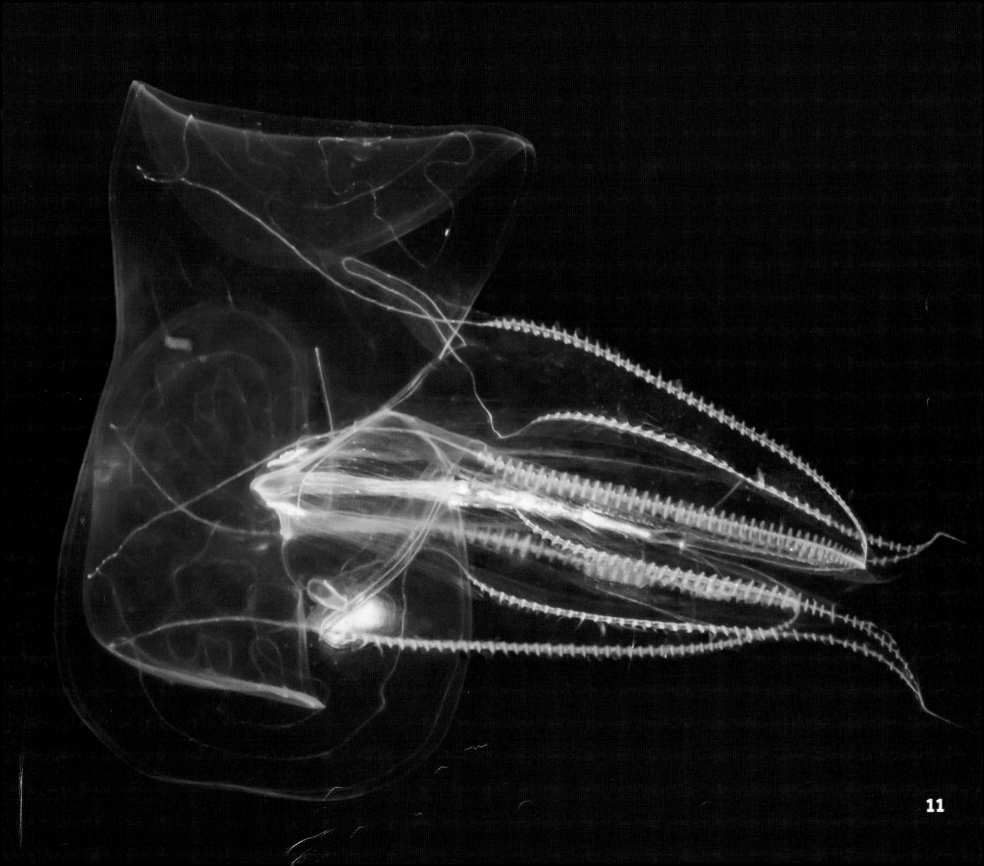

Jellyfish do not have bones.
They have soft bodies shaped
like bells or umbrellas.
They open and close their
bodies to move.

Finding food

Jellyfish have many tentacles. The tentacles sting prey with poison. Once they are stung, the prey cannot swim away.

The tentacles pull the prey
into the jellyfish's mouth.
Jellyfish eat fish and plankton.

Life cycle

Female jellyfish make eggs.

The eggs later grow into polyps.

Polyps live on the seabed.

19

Young jellyfish grow
from the polyps.
They break away and
move on their own.
In a few weeks, they
become adult jellyfish.

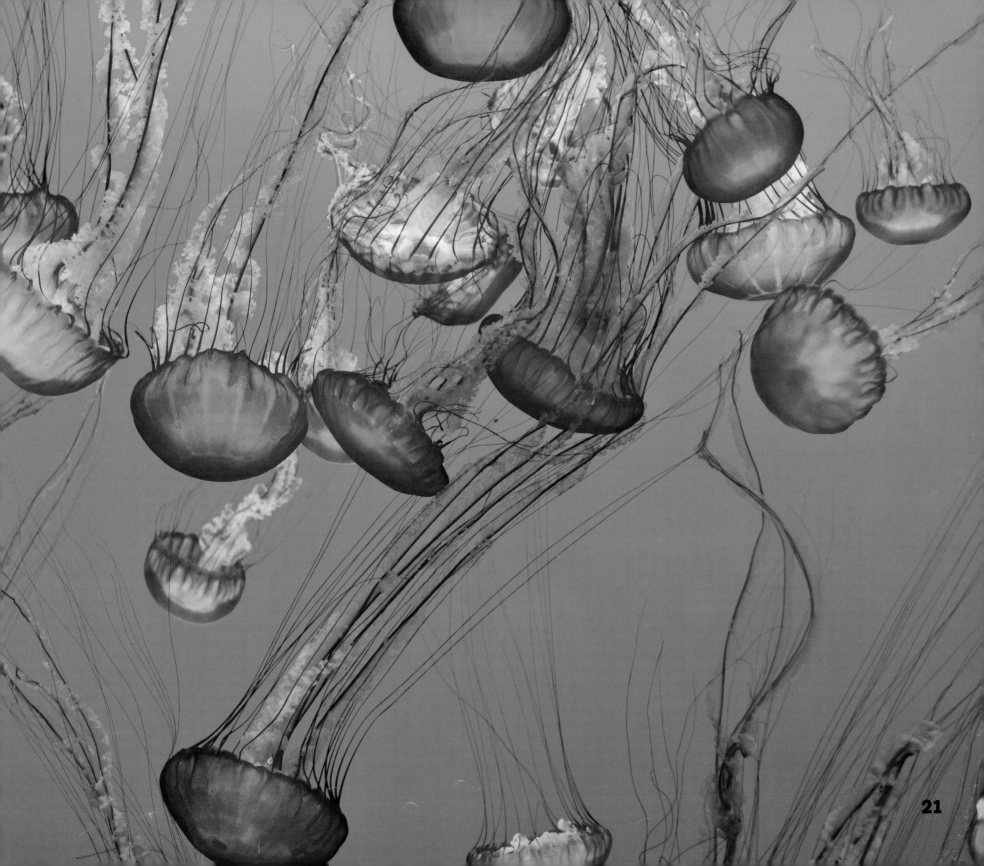

Glossary

plankton small or tiny animals and plants that drift or float in seas and oceans

poison substance that can kill or harm an animal or human

polyp jellyfish at the stage of development during which it lives on the seabed

prey animal hunted by another animal for food

tentacle long, flexible body part used for moving, feeling and grabbing

Read more

Jellyfish (A Day in the Life: Sea Animals), Louise Spilsbury (Raintree, 2011)

Sea Animals (Animals in their Habitats), Sian Smith (Raintree, 2014)

Usborne First Encyclopedia of Seas and Oceans, Jane Chisholm (Usborne Publishing, 2011)

Websites

www.bbc.co.uk/nature/life/Jellyfish
Watch videos and find out more about jellyfish.

www.national-aquarium.co.uk/50-fun-facts
Fun facts about sea and ocean life.

Index

bodies 12

bones 12

colouring 10

eggs 18

food 14, 16

habitat 6

polyps 18, 20

size 8

tentacles 14, 16

young 20